Original title:
Whales in the Wind

Copyright © 2025 Creative Arts Management OÜ
All rights reserved.

Author: Gabriel Kingsley
ISBN HARDBACK: 978-1-80587-239-9
ISBN PAPERBACK: 978-1-80587-709-7

Lifting Spirits of the Sea

In the depths where the big ones play,
They munch on krill all day.
With tails that swish and splashes wide,
They make the ocean their joyful ride.

Up they leap, a mighty show,
Belly flops cause quite a glow.
Seagulls chuckle, they dive and dip,
As bubbly giants take a trip.

They sing a tune, a deep bass sound,
To tickle the fish that swim around.
While dancing currents swirl about,
They seem to giggle, there's no doubt.

With fins so wide, they wave hello,
To curious boats in a row.
A splash of fun, and off they go,
Making waves with their hulking show!

Tides of Tranquility

Belly flop from sea to sea,
They glide like stars, oh so free.
Splashing water, what a sight,
Making fishy friends at night.

Their songs ring out, a joyous tune,
While sea gulls dance and swoon.
With jets of spray, they say hi,
To boats that pass and give a sigh.

Celestial Migrations

Up they go, a big splash dance,
In the air, they take a chance.
Spinning 'round like they're in a show,
A circus act down below.

From ocean floor to sky so bright,
The crowd all cheers, what a delight!
They flap their fins, a comic scene,
As fish gawk wide-eyed and keen.

Giants Beneath the Horizon

Monsters leaping, it's quite absurd,
They play tag with the wavy herd.
With glee they twist, then dive so deep,
Sending sharks to take a leap!

Underwater, they hold their breath,
While jellyfish dance near their depth.
Navigating like pros, it seems,
They dream of tacos and ice cream.

Chasing Breezes

With fins like sails, they catch the breeze,
Doing flips with effortless ease.
They giggle loud, in blubbery tones,
As dolphins dance on sandy stones.

A leap here, a splash there, what a spree,
Floating 'round like it's pure glee.
They shout, "Catch us if you can!"
With bubbles bursting, isn't that grand?

Riding Waves

On the crest of waves they ride,
A slippery, happy, ocean slide.
With every swoosh and swish they take,
They tickle fish and make them quake.

Round and round like merry-goes,
The ocean's laughter, everyone knows.
"Whee!" they call, "Let's race a boat!"
As seals applaud from a nearby float.

Ocean's Breath

In the sea, where laughter churns,
A fishy joke, the tide returns.
Blowholes puff like birthday cakes,
Bubbles dance, oh what a prank!

Splashing down with comic flair,
Seagulls squawk, polka-dot their hair.
Tails wagging like dogs at play,
Who needs a circus? Come this way!

A flip, a splash, they steal the scene,
With wiggles and jiggles, oh so keen.
A dance of splashes, fin and glee,
What a laugh, come dive with me!

So here's to those who swim and sing,
With tales so tall, they make us swing.
Ocean's breath, a playful jest,
In salty waves, we find our rest.

Gentle Giants: A Love Letter

To my gentle giant, oh so grand,
With blubber hugs and tiny hands.
Your heart, a drum, beats full of cheer,
In ocean depths, I hold you near.

Your friendly spouts, like kisses blown,
A love that's vast, and rarely shown.
You swim alone, yet know my call,
In your presence, I feel so small.

Oh, how you frolic, in gleeful loops,
With silly snorts and belly whoops.
Each playful breach, a joke in light,
You make my days a pure delight!

So here's my letter, from sea to shore,
To the biggest love, whom I adore.
With every wave, I send this cheer,
Forever yours, my dear, my dear!

Off the Coast of Dreams

Dreams set sail on waves so bright,
Where giants play, and chase the light.
Their shadows dance beneath the blue,
With tails that tell a tale or two.

A splash and a giggle, the ocean sighs,
As they leap and whirl beneath the skies.
In this aquatic joy parade,
They twirl and spin; no need for shade.

A waltz with dolphins, a jig with rays,
In frothy glamour, they spend their days.
Whale-sized pranks, a friendly tease,
Floating merrily, just to please.

So off we go, where dreams collide,
With laughter bubbling, side by side.
In this ocean vast, together we'll float,
In a world where fun and dreams remote.

Floating Elysium

In floating realms where bubbles burst,
The giants giggle, oh, how they thirst!
For seaweed snacks and jellyfish pies,
Their tasty treats bring joy to the skies.

With grace like dancers, they glide and spin,
A circus show beneath their fin.
In this happy haven, smiles abound,
With tickles and splashes, love is found.

From ocean's depths to sunny beaches,
They share their laughter, oh how it reaches!
Creating joy with each gentle wave,
In this playful tide, we misbehave.

Oh, floating Elysium, delighting our hearts,
With every splash, a new smile starts.
Join the dance as we sing along,
In the realm of joy, we all belong.

Silence of the Undersea Giants

In the ocean's deep domain,
A fishy joke doth reign,
'The giant has lost his hat!' they say,
As bubbles rise and drift away.

With flippers flapping all around,
They dance and jive without a sound,
A secret rave for those who swim,
While mermaids laugh with gills quite grim.

Gigantic shadows cast a grin,
When krill-titans start to spin,
Their blubber bounces with delight,
As they glide through the sea at night.

In schools where mischief takes its hold,
They trade bad puns like grains of gold,
Tales of gales and splashes bold,
Those jolly giants never old!

Secrets of the Tides

In the waves, such secrets dwell,
Like a fish that learned to spell,
'I need some salt, a splash of cheer,'
It scribbles bright, so crystal clear.

The sea's a place for funny tricks,
Where barnacles perform slick kicks,
With starfish chess on the sandy floor,
It's laughter that the tides adore.

As currents swirl and whirl around,
The splash of jokes is quite profound,
Fish are giggling, while crabs debate,
'Who caught the biggest fish? Just wait!'

So join the fun beneath the waves,
Where laughter echoes, and mischief braves,
With seaweed wigs and clams that sing,
The underwater joy is a truly wild thing!

Beneath the Surface Skies

Beneath the waves, what sights to see,
A turtle wearing shades like me!
With barnacles all stuck in place,
He winks and grins with utmost grace.

The dolphin jokes with effortless ease,
'Why did the fish swim back with the breeze?'
'To find its scales in fashion's fray,
It missed the boat and wanted to play!'

With bubbles floating like balloons,
They throw a party beneath the moons,
The octopus dances with eight left feet,
While corals sway to the rhythmic beat.

So take a dive and join the cheer,
With jellyfish lighting up the sphere,
For beneath the surface, joy resides,
With laughter and antics like roaring tides!

Glimpses of the Horizon

At dawn, the horizon starts to glow,
Sea turtles frolic in a comedic show,
'The sun is too bright!' they dive and swirl,
Avoiding rays with a flip and twirl.

A playful splash sends fish on a spree,
'Can you catch me?' they giggle with glee,
Seagulls join in, taking a bite,
'Race you to shore!' – oh, what a sight!

As waves race forth and tumble back,
Dolphins leap high on their joyful track,
With fins a-flailing, they sing their song,
Convinced they're the best—can't be wrong!

So look to the sea, embrace the scene,
Where laughter bubbles and life is keen,
For glimpses of joy, oh so divine,
Are found where the ocean and humor intertwine!

Glimmering Trails on Water

In the splashy dance, they glide and sway,
Tickling the tides in their own silly way,
Belly flops, they jest, with a joyful splash,
Making waves of laughter with each playful crash.

Glimmers like silver, they twirl and spin,
As fishes giggle, saying, "Let the fun begin!"
With bubble-blowing antics atop the blue,
The ocean's comedians put on a show for you.

Jumping high, they wear crowns of foam,
In the kingdom of salt, they're right at home,
A fluke here, a wink there, oh what a scene,
In the watery circus, they're the clowns of the marine!

So grab your snorkels, join in their prank,
With every gurgle and giggle in rank,
For when they gather, the sea becomes bright,
With joy-making giants, filling day and night.

Blue Giants in Reverie

In dreams, they swim with hats made of foam,
Winking at seagulls, claiming the ocean their home,
They twirl and they whirl in the sun's warm glow,
With a wink and a twist, putting on quite the show.

In bubble-filled ballets, they leap and prance,
Wearing turtleneck sweaters, they start a big dance,
All the fish cheer, giving a loud cheer,
For the giants in blue bring joy far and near.

With ice cream cones topped, they glide on their backs,
Shooting silly grins, leaving friends in cracks,
Chasing each other, in a splashy embrace,
Mirth and delight splashing every space.

So when you gaze, and see that big fin,
Know there's laughter a-swelling deep within,
From fantastical dreams that they often weave,
The blue giants dance, and make us believe.

Windborne Echoes

Hear the chuckles from deep in the sea,
As breezes carry jokes, amusing as can be,
With tails that flip, they tickle the breeze,
Creating echoes that bounce with ease.

"Catch me if you can!" one tumbles about,
With a splash of bright bubbles, there's laughter throughout,
They toss and they tangle in rambunctious delight,
These merry ocean jesters, both joyful and bright.

In the gentle swirls, their giggles take flight,
Tickling the surfaces, oh what a sight!
With voices like songs, they serenade the sky,
In hilarious harmony, they leap and they fly.

So if you feel wind that carries a snicker,
Know it's the ocean pals playing their flicker,
With each gust of joy, they honestly send,
The whimsical laughter that has no end.

Celestial Songlines

Under starry skies, they sing and they hum,
Crafting melodies where all creatures come,
With tunes that twist like the waves' gentle roll,
These cosmic comedians fill the night with soul.

Floating like clouds on a whimsical spree,
They burp out constellations, just for you and me,
With winks made of stardust, they weave in and out,
Making merry mischief with a sticker-covered shout.

So tip your hats to the giant blue friends,
Who dance through the dark until daylight blends,
With laughter like bubbles rising up high,
They're the jesters of night, beneath the divine sky.

In this cosmic ballet, they prance, wiggle, and sway,
With chuckles and joy to brighten the way,
For when the night calls, join their playful song,
And in the universe's circus, know that you belong.

Nautical Reverie

A cow jumped high over the moon,
On a boat that blew bubbles in June.
The fish wore hats, sipping tea,
While crumpets danced, wild and free.

A parrot pilfered the captain's snack,
Sailed with seagulls, on a snack attack.
The waves giggled; they couldn't resist,
As the crew of oddballs formed their tryst.

The octopus played the piano well,
As the dolphins sang, a jolly bell.
Turtle tangoed with a swift star,
In a warm embrace under the radar.

And when the sun set, all let out a cheer,
For they knew tomorrow, fun would appear!
With shells for trumpets, and foam for flip,
Life on the ocean, a comical trip!

The Whispering Horizon

An otter hosted a talent show,
With synchronized swimming, putting on a glow.
The seals clapped their flippers with glee,
While clumsy crabs shuffled in a spree.

The horizon whispered silly jokes,
To a circle of quacking, giggling folks.
With laughs that rolled like the tide's embrace,
Joy floated around, a bubbly place.

A mermaid sang off-key for fun,
While the whale puppets spun in the sun.
With fruit salad hats and jellybean shoes,
They paraded around, spreading the blues.

The sun and moon, best friends in the sky,
Joined in the laughter, oh me, oh my!
For every wave brought fresh giggles anew,
In this whimsical world, where dreams come true!

Celestial Navigators

Two stars played chess on a night so clear,
While comets traded tales, drawing near.
Space clowns juggled planets with glee,
As aliens danced to galactic spree.

An astronaut slipped on a cosmic slide,
With planets as pillows, where dreams reside.
Rockets zoomed past with glittering trails,
While space whales shared their interstellar tales.

A satellite caught a star's funny fart,
Sending giggles that tickled the heart.
With black holes laughing, and meteors spry,
The universe chuckled, oh my, oh my!

With laughter ringing from star to star,
Navigators float in this world bizarre.
Through a cosmos gleeful and ever so bright,
Joy awaits in the shimmering night!

Boundless Spirits

A jolly sea sponge wore a bright bowtie,
Telling tall tales that made time fly.
The starfish tapped their sand-filled feet,
Embracing the rhythm of the ocean's beat.

A lobster played tricks, trying to dance,
With jellyfish swirling in a bubbly trance.
Crabs joined in with their sideways strut,
While clam shells clacked, oh what a rut!

In a barrel of laughs, they tumbled and swirled,\nAs sea
urchins giggled in their spiked world.
The salty breeze carried chuckles all day,
In this sea of laughter, come out and play!

As night fell, glowworms sparkled so bright,
Underwater disco, a marvelous sight.
With every splash and a tickle of fins,
Boundless spirits find joy, and the laughter begins!

Whispering Fins

In the sea, they prank the fish,
Blowing bubbles, making a wish.
With flippers flipped, they swim about,
Spinning tales that make us shout.

Their laughter echoes, quite a cheer,
Beneath the waves, it's crystal clear.
They frolic and play, such silly sights,
As they bounce in the ocean's heights.

Skies of the Deep Blue

Above, they leap, a comic show,
In the sunlight's gleaming glow.
With tails like trumpets, they make a sound,
Splashing water all around.

They chat and giggle, what a blast,
In their kingdom, sails are cast.
With charming grins and joyful spins,
They dance like kings, oh where to begin?

Call of the Ocean Spirits

Hear the giggles from afar,
As they joke beneath the star.
With every splash, a laugh is heard,
What a funny, flappy bird!

They sing of tides, and winds that jive,
With rhythmic beats, they come alive.
Twirling 'round, making waves,
In a comedic whirl, the ocean graves.

Dance of the Marine Behemoths

In the sea, they sway and spin,
Chasing bubbles stuck in their fin.
With goofy flips and a playful roar,
They churn the water, who could ask for more?

Jesting at currents, swirling with delight,
Making quick turns, oh what a sight!
As they twirl and swirl, the ocean grins,
For the fun is endless, where laughter begins.

Mysterious Melodies

In the ocean's great expanse, they glide,
Singing tunes, not meant to hide.
With a belly flop and a splashy twist,
They humor the waves with a watery fist.

Bubble-blowers of the briny deep,
Making fish giggle while they sleep.
A bouncy joke in the sea's grand tale,
Dancing in circles, a comical whale.

With a flick of a fin, they make their mark,
Playing tag with a passing shark.
Their laughter echoes from near to far,
Like a bubbly sitcom starring a star.

As frolicsome friends dive down below,
They send up giggles, a cheerful show.
In the salty air, with joy they'll thrive,
Mysterious melodies keep them alive.

Spirits of the Sea

Beneath the waves, they swing and sway,
Spirits of the sea, brightening the day.
With their silly winks and splashing play,
They turn dull moments into a cabaret.

Jumping and jiggling, tails held high,
They wave goodbye like they dare you to try.
Message in bubbles, a giggle is sent,
As they twirl and tumble, their time is well-spent.

Blowing bubbles in the ocean's breeze,
Squeaking their jokes like a sailor's tease.
With flippers slapping the surface above,
They play pranks on boats, filled with love.

As the sun sets, they chant their tune,
Singing sonnets to the sleepy moon.
Spirits so bright in a world of blue,
Life is a joke, and they're laughing too.

Guardians of the Salty Air

With oversized smiles, they rule the tides,
Guardians of laughter where mischief resides.
They twirl and whirl in a breezy ballet,
Keeping the ocean's frowns far at bay.

Popping up high with a splashy cheer,
Dancing like clowns, they spread the good cheer.
Their giant grins light the ocean's stage,
Each leap and dive, a laugh out of rage.

Hooting and hollering in frothy delight,
They tease the seagulls from morning till night.
In a merry jig, through salt they sway,
Guardians of fun, in their magical way.

So raise your glass to these friendly giants,
With their cheeky smiles and buoyant defiance.
In the salty air where giggles persist,
They bubble with joy, too good to resist.

Echoing Through the Surf

Echoes of laughter ride every wave,
From creatures who dance and love to be brave.
With each playful splash, they send forth their tune,
Making even the sunbeam chuckle in June.

Leaping with glee, in the sparkling brine,
They twirl like dervishes, feeling divine.
Comedic acts in this theater of blue,
Where every rich laugh feels fresh and new.

As the tide rolls in, they sprout silly tales,
Casting their caps like mischievous sails.
Chasing the sunset, they flip and dive,
Echoes of joy, keeping dreams alive.

With a flick and a flop, they splatter the air,
Crafting cool jokes that none can compare.
As echoes resound through the crashing surf,
These gaggling giants remind us of mirth.

Whispers of the Abyss

In the depth where shadows lurk,
Sea creatures twerk and go berserk.
Bubbles rise with giggling glee,
As sardines dance, oh so carefree.

An octopus, with flair so bright,
Tries to juggle with all its might.
But all that's seen is ink and splash,
While fish all snicker, what a crash!

Turtles lounging, hats on their heads,
Making puns 'bout days in beds.
Crabs throw parties with goofy tunes,
Inviting everyone, even raccoons!

Down deep where laughter is the show,
Every flick of fin gets a glow.
They frolic, play, beneath the tides,
In this ocean of glee, no one hides.

Timeless Journeys on the Surface

A bearded seal wearing a tie,
Floats on a log, waves 'hello' to the sky.
Sipping tea while drifting away,
Baloons tied on knobs—what a display!

Dolphins trade jokes, quick as a flash,
One tells a quip, the rest all smash.
With every leap, they spin and twirl,
Making the surf dance, giving a whirl.

Seagulls caw, telling tales of the shore,
With exaggerated wigs, they beg for more.
They giggle and flop, never a care,
Chasing the waves, through salty air.

While the sun sets, pinks and golds,
The fish all gather, shimmery folds.
Painting pictures with fins so grand,
As laughter echoes, across the sand.

Messengers of the Deep

A fish with glasses reads the news,
Spreading tales of the ocean views.
"Did you hear the one 'bout the clam who sang?"
Echoes bubble, as sardines hang.

Starfish wearing boots, strut in a line,
Boasting of adventures, all can be fine.
Digging through sand, with giggles abound,
Their pranks last all night, in joy profound.

Anemones whisper, what secrets they share,
While flounders freeze for a silly dare.
Tickling each other with gills and fins,
As the echo of laughter, the sea spins.

The coral reefs light up at night,
With disco balls and colorful sight.
Every creature joins, the party's begun,
In this realm where jokes flow like sun.

Floating Dreams on Currents

A walrus in shades floats with style,
Sipping on smoothies, he grins all the while.
Discussing fashion with fish so sleek,
While otters try to sneak a peak.

Hippos in rafts, heading downstream,
With loud whoops and giggles, oh what a dream!
They race to the finish with splashes and fun,
Laughing out loud as they soak in the sun.

Jellyfish glow like disco lights,
Dancing to tunes in the ocean nights.
With every pulsating, they sway with glee,
Turns out, they're quite the sight to see.

Starry-eyed pirates search for the gold,
But it's jelly-filled donuts they often behold.
Instead of treasures, they laugh and play,
In this whimsical world, forever they'll stay.

Echoes of Ocean Giants

In the depths they frolic, with glee,
Doing belly flops for all to see.
A splash here, a splash there,
Who knew sea critters had flair?

With flip-flops made of kelp and sea,
They dance like drifters, wild and free.
Hurling seaweed like it's confetti,
What a sight—so loud and yet so petty!

Guffaws resonate through the blue,
As barnacles giggle in a crew.
They tell tall tales of joyful strife,
Making waves that cut like a knife.

The show's not over until they dive,
These leviathans sure know to jive.
Bubbles float up, laughter in tow,
The party continues, never slow!

Serenade of the Deep

Underwater karaoke takes flight,
With tunes that spark like starlight.
A crowd of fish sings, 'Ooh la la!',
To the beat of a crab playing guitar.

Bubbles pop like champagne at noon,
As octopi join with a funky tune.
Jellyfish sway with hypnotic grace,
In this underwater music space.

A clownfish dons a funny hat,
While anemones dance—how about that?
The audience roars, their scales a-glimmer,
As the beats drop, the lights get dimmer.

The maestro, a whale who knows it well,
Spins tall tales within his shell.
As notes escape on currents strong,
This deep-sea concert won't be long!

Breath of the Blue

In the blue, they take a breath,
Leaving bubbles that smell like a wreath.
With goofy grins and silly spouts,
They charm the coral with joyous shouts.

Swimming in circles, they spin and swirl,
Each one thinks they're quite the pearl.
With hugs from anemones and tickles from fish,
Their laughter echoes—a bubbly wish.

Tales of treasure from sunken ships,
Delightfully shared with playful quips.
A dolphin giggles, 'I found a shoe!'
While a starfish thinks it'd fit him too.

As the ocean hums a lively tune,
They play together beneath the moon.
With each splash, a memory made,
In the deep where fun won't fade.

Songs of the Silver Sea

A silver surfer riding high,
Takes a leap, oh my, oh my!
He flips and flops with ocean grace,
Bringing silly smiles across the face.

The gulls squawk tunes atop the waves,
While singing mermaids build their caves.
Fiddling crabs keep time with claws,
As laughter dances, breaking laws.

In a treasure chest, a party waits,
With sparkling shells and tasty plates.
Jellyfish juggling, what a scene,
Life's a beach on this silver screen.

As twilight falls and flickers fade,
The ocean giggles, no charades.
With each wave, they spread their cheer,
In this grand ballet—no need for fear!

Harmony in Aqua

In the ocean's deep, they sing a song,
With gurgling giggles, they splash along.
Bubbles rise higher, tickling the air,
Fish start to dance, without a care.

All the sea creatures join in the fun,
Jellyfish jiving under the sun.
Octopuses twist, their limbs in a whirl,
As if they're part of some underwater swirl.

Seaweed sways, doing a funky groove,
Turtles do cartwheels, it's time to move.
The barnacles hum on a rocky stage,
While crabs give out autographs as a rage.

Tails Telling Tales

With a flick and a flop, a story's begun,
A whale with a tail claims he's the one.
He's seen legends rise from the ocean street,
While dolphins dive down in a giggling feat.

"Tales of the caves where the sea-monsters creep,
And seagulls that steal all the treasure they keep!"
Laughter erupts from the plankton below,
"Is that why our taco shells sparkle and glow?"

A clam starts to clap, not with both his hands,
But with his two shells, as the crowd understands.
The fish sway in rhythm, each story a shout,
In the merriment, no one cares to pout.

Glide of the Enormous

A giant once glided through waters so wide,
With such a big grin, he took life in stride.
His buddies all joked as he made quite a splash,
"Look at him go, he's a whale of a mash!"

He swirled and he twirled, creating a fuss,
Sending squids flying in a bright, blue gust.
"Careful!" cried turtles, who dodged with a laugh,
"Don't take out the boats with your oceanic staff!"

As the breeze blew sweet, the sea started to cheer,
With giggles and shouts that echoed near.
Under the sun, they all laughed in glee,
The colossal wave-maker, wild and free.

Waves of the Great Ones

In the depths where the giants hold court with a grin,
The waves roll with laughter, a bubbly spin.
Each crest a new riddle, each trough a big joke,
Even the seaweed lets out a soft poke.

Splashing and dashing, they're all in good cheer,
The currents are pulling, as if to draw near.
Nautical nonsense, beneath the moonlight,
With jokes that transpire till the end of the night.

And when morning dawns, with a shimmer and shine,
The ocean will giggle, proclaiming, "You're mine!"
So raise your flippers, dance about in the foam,
For in this great sea, we all call it home.

Gentle Giants in Flight

In ocean's dance, they twirl and sway,
With splashes loud, they laugh and play.
They ride the waves, with flips and flops,
Their joy erupts, oh how it hops!

With breezy tales, they swim so free,
Like floating kites, just wait and see.
They tease the gulls, with breezy grace,
A hungry fin, a quick embrace.

Through seaweed fields, they glide with glee,
In playful arcs of jubilee.
Bubble-blowing, what a sight!
Dining on plankton, pure delight!

Round and round, they turn and dive,
Making the ocean come alive.
With gentle roars, they sing a tune,
As sunbeams dance 'neath the bright moon.

Breaths Beneath the Breeze

With every exhale, a splash they make,
Silly bubbles, a frothy lake.
They puff and puff, like giant toys,
Their underwater fun brings endless joys.

Gliding past, they steal the show,
Casting shadows, a curious glow.
With faces bright, and tails that flip,
They cruise along on every trip.

Beneath the surface, they find their mirth,
Each gulp a giggle, a belly-laugh birth.
Their buoyant bodies bounce through light,
In a canvas painted pure delight.

As waves tickle, they chirp and squeal,
Oh, such mischief, what a steal!
In this grand ocean, they find the groove,
Floating and frolicking, forever in a move.

Majesty on the Current

With a twist and a wiggle, they glide so grand,
Majestic dancers in deep water's band.
They throw all their weight into frothy leaps,
While schools of fish take little peeks.

In swirling currents, they spin around,
Tickling the surface with not a sound.
With flukes like sails, there's joy to behold,
Their laughter carried on winds so bold.

They prance and play in a watery maze,
Crafting stories in playful ways.
A belly flop here, a splash there,
The ocean chuckles, free as air.

Bright-eyed creatures of the sea,
With hearts like giggles, forever carefree.
They reign sharp currents, like kings in blue,
Majesty they bring in every hue.

Celestial Creatures of the Deep

In the deep sea's cradle, they swim and shine,
Like comets racing, oh how divine!
With sparkly splashes, a cosmic dance,
They whirl like stars in a frothy prance.

Glimmers of laughter echo all around,
As each mighty leap makes a joyful sound.
They poke at the surface, with fins that twirl,
Making the ocean their playful swirl.

Cosmic antics beneath the crest,
A game of chase, they never rest.
With bubbles bright, and beacons of glee,
They fill the blue with endless spree.

So let the waves carry their giddy smiles,
As they roam the waters, chasing miles.
In splashes and giggles, they cascade free,
Celestial wonders beneath the sea.

The Great Dance of Sea and Sky

In the blue, a splash and swish,
A great big tail, an ocean wish.
The gulls all laugh, they see the show,
As fish below in bubbles blow.

The skies are wide, the waves are bold,
With lumbering grace, so bright and cold.
The breeze, it tickles, the surf it winks,
While sea folks ponder, and the sunshine blinks.

They twirl and twist, with quite a flair,
A mariner's giggle fills the air.
The ocean's floor, a dance floor grand,
Where fins and flippers high five on sand.

So raise a glass to the sea's delight,
The frolicking fun from day to night.
In waters deep, their laughter rings,
As waves collide and the seagulls sing.

Whispers of Ocean Giants

Beneath the waves, where secrets dwell,
The big ones giggle, oh what a spell!
With every splash and playful breeze,
They share their jokes with cheeky ease.

One says, 'I've conquered waves so tall,'
While juggling fish, they never fall.
The krill all chuckle, a skit unfolds,
As tales of the deep, their heart it holds.

The barnacles clap, the sea anemones cheer,
'Did you hear the one about the sea beer?'
They swirl and sway, embracing the thrill,
These gentle giants give us all a chill.

With blubbery laughter, the ocean sparks,
From whale-sized humor to tiny larks.
The coastal waves join in the jest,
In watery worlds, we find our best.

Transcendence Above the Waves

Floating high, a splashy sight,
They leap with glee, a pure delight.
A saucy wink, a twist in air,
They pirouette without a care.

The wind weaves tunes of frothy fun,
As water dancers play and run.
With every bounce, the sea does sing,
While seabirds watch from flapping wing.

Oh what a sight, a comical spree,
A game of tag from sea to sea.
In dwindling light, a splash of cheer,
As foamy waves say, "Come join here!"

So glide through life, with laughter bright,
In playful arcs, soar out of sight.
For up in the air, we're all one team,
On this funny oceanic dream.

Oceanic Wishes in Flight

On a gust of whim, they start to roam,
With hefty grace, they call it home.
Each flip a giggle, each glide a glee,
As sea swells echo with wild bonhomie.

The dolphins cheer, the turtles smile,
While hopping fish leap in style.
With breezy antics and silly play,
These floating jesters brighten the day.

They wish on tides, as bubbles rise,
With each gurgled chuckle, a surprise.
The ocean brims with fun galore,
As salty laughter fills the shore.

So here's to the sea, where dreams take flight,
With every splash, they rule the night.
In watery realms of joy and mirth,
The laughter echoes, a place of birth.

Echoing Calls Across the Expanse

In the blue, they play and splash,
Giant fish with a funny dash.
They sing songs that wobble and jive,
Making the seagulls laugh and dive.

Bubbles rise like laughter's cheer,
Echoing wide, oh so near.
A dance of tails in ocean's sway,
Who knew fish could feel this way?

Their laughter fills the ocean's dome,
A booming giggle, a joyful home.
With every dive, a chuckling sound,
In their world, pure silliness is found.

So next time you see them glide,
Remember their antics, full of pride.
These gentle giants, with hums galore,
Bring joy to all, forevermore.

Mystic Movements of Ocean Souls

Beneath the waves, they twirl and tease,
Swimming in circles, with so much ease.
They wink their eyes, and with a grin,
Pull off stunts that make you spin.

A leap, a spin, a dive so neat,
They make it look like such a treat.
With flippers flapping like happy sails,
In their world of jumps, laughter prevails.

Wiggling tails wave 'hello' to the sun,
Tickling sea turtles just for fun.
With every splash, the ocean's bright,
As mystic swimmers dance through night.

In a watery jig, they create a fuss,
A comedy show aboard their bus.
So join the fun, let laughter roll,
With these ocean souls, so full of soul.

The Rise and Fall of Legends

In the depths, a tale unfolds,
Of titans who were never old.
With blubbery bodies, they float and dive,
In the ocean's tale, they're so alive.

Their epic battles, quite absurd,
The biggest splash, you've surely heard.
With flops and flails, they take the stage,
Crafting legends that never age.

From the great abyss, they rise and dip,
Their joyous antics, a comic trip.
With wide-open mouths, they guffaw and cheer,
Making the sea life laugh, oh dear!

In rhythm and rhyme, they conquer the blue,
Legendary figures, with jokes anew.
Once fierce and grand, now just for play,
They rule the depths in the silliest way.

Horizons of the Gentle Titans

Across the waves, they drift and sway,
Gentle titans at play all day.
With a puff of air, they blow a kiss,
Creating rainbows of watery bliss.

They swim with grace, oh what a sight,
Dancing in sunbeams, sheer delight.
With every leap, laughter shakes the sea,
The ocean's joy is wild and free.

Belly flops and silly spins,
These gentle giants know how to win.
Their massive forms create whirls of fun,
As they play tag with the glowing sun.

So let's not forget their playful spree,
In the vastness, they dance with glee.
With every splash, they light the sky,
Horizons smile as the titans fly.

Tidal Echoes

In the splashy dance of the sea,
Creatures leap with glee, you see.
They twist and twirl, so spry and light,
Making waves on this comical night.

Fish in bow ties, all dressed to thrill,
Performing flips, what a crazy skill!
The crowd of crabs clap with delight,
As starfish juggle, a hilarious sight.

Jellyfish roll like a bouncy ball,
Making even the clams chuckle and sprawl.
With a cheer so loud, they all declare,
Who knew the ocean had such flair!

As the tides crash with a giggle and grin,
We laugh as the antics of sea life begin.
In the grand amphitheater of the brine,
Nature's comedy is simply divine!

Ethereal Backdrops of the Ocean

Bubbles rise like confetti in the air,
A dolphin's laugh is echoing everywhere.
With fantastical flips in the sunlit bay,
You can't help but smile at their playful display.

Octopuses painting with ink on display,
Drawing cartoons of the fish's ballet.
Seahorses prance in a fabulous style,
In this underwater circus, they charm with a smile.

With anemone wigs and seaweed ties,
Every critter twirls as the ocean replies.
Turtles in shades are the kings of the show,
Slide on the waves with a hip little flow.

As the sun dips down and the colors ignite,
The ocean's a stage, making laughter unite.
So join in the fun, take a peek through the foam,
In this wacky wonderland, we all find a home!

Celestial Winged Wonders

With a splash, the big guys take flight,
Leaping from waves, oh what a sight!
Spouting stories of where they have been,
In the air, they twirl like a whimsical scene.

A pelican laughs with its beak in the blue,
Dropping snacks for the fishes, too.
The gulls all join in the playful ballet,
As seagulls honk jokes that brighten the day.

Under the bright sun, the pelagic stars,
Dance with the turtles and leisurely cars.
Who knew such hilarity lurked in the bay?
A fleet of fins formed a cabaret.

So float on the breeze, let your spirit unwind,
In this carnival of laughter, joy you'll find.
With wings and fins breaking free from their chains,
It's a party of giggles, where fun never wanes!

The Song of Depths

Deep in the blue, where the jesters glide,
A chorus of giggles begins to coincide.
They sway to the rhythm of gurgles and waves,
A symphony of laughter from the ocean's caves.

The grumpy old grouper rolls his big eyes,
As a clam starts singing, much to his surprise.
According to legend, it's lost waves from old,
In this aquatic soiree, tales are retold.

The trumpetfish toots and the heron takes flight,
While eels do the cha-cha, which is quite a sight.
Shellfish are cheering, and they clink their shells,
As pufferfish puff out giggles and yells.

So come join the fun, as the waves serenade,
The ocean's own humor is never betrayed.
In this symphony of joy, where laughter's the key,
Let's dance to the song of the deep, carefree!

Drifting with the Sea's Heart

Bubbles pop and splash around,
As sea giants dance without a sound.
They swish and swirl, what a sight,
Oh, do they have a knack for flight!

A turtle waves, looks quite perplexed,
While fishes giggle, completely vexed.
'Why's he leaping? In a play?'
A dolphin grins, 'He's here to stay!'

The captain's hat is far too big,
It flops around like a seaweed twig.
They flip and flop, oh what a race,
In salty air, they find their space.

With every splash, the sun will wink,
And all aboard forgot to think.
In the heart of the ocean, they roam,
Finding joy in the blue, their home.

Song of the Leviathans

Beneath the waves, they hum a tune,
A bubble choir beneath the moon.
Their voices echo, deep and wide,
Like underwater karaoke, there's no need to hide!

One goes high, and one goes low,
Singing songs of things they know.
A crab joins in with a clippy clap,
While a starfish winks, 'Enjoy the rap!'

Giant tails make waves like a dance,
With flippers flapping, they take a chance.
However, a clam, with a twisty grin,
Said, 'Join the chorus, let the fun begin!'

And through the laughter, joy and sound,
They serenade the ocean round.
With every note, they blend and sway,
What a silly, splashing, song-filled day!

Currents and Caresses

Oh, look at them, with grace they glide,
Like fluffy clouds in ocean's tide.
With fluke and fin, they spin and twirl,
Creating whirlpools that make you swirl!

The jellyfish join with a shimmy shake,
While seahorses groove, oh for goodness' sake!
They wear tiny hats, quite snug and neat,
As bubbles bob in this festive beat.

An octopus plays on a saxophone,
Playing jazzy tunes all on its own.
With ink in hand, it draws a scene,
A silly shark dancing, oh so keen!

They wave goodbye with a flip and a splash,
These marvels of the ocean, quite the bash!
With currents drawing them out to play,
They remind us all to embrace each day.

Shadows of the Sea's Titans

In the depths where shadows creep,
Big fishes joke while little ones sleep.
They play peek-a-boo with the rays of light,
Looking for giggles, what a delight!

A kraken moans, 'Not again with this!',
While minnows flee from a treble kiss.
With tentacles flinging, they can't keep still,
Each splash bringing laughter, a watery thrill.

Amidst the bubbles and gentle sway,
The narwhal prances, brightening the day.
With a silly smile, it shows its horn,
Making everyone laugh until they're worn!

As they cavort in salty abyss,
Their whimsical antics are pure bliss.
In shadows of titans, they find the gold,
In stories of laughter, forever told.

Under Currents of Blue

Bubbles rise, a giggle stream,
Fish dance in a wobbly dream.
Waves that twist and swirl with glee,
Beneath the surface, so carefree.

Splashing sounds that tickle the air,
Sea critters joining in the flair.
Flipping tails in a playful tease,
Making jellyfish laugh with ease.

Barnacles join in the fun parade,
Wobbling along, quite unafraid.
Eels crack jokes with a slithery grin,
While sea cucumbers join in the spin.

Aerial Ballet of the Giants

Synchronized leaps, a grand display,
Fins waving hello in a breezy ballet.
Giant bodies just flopping around,
As seagulls swoop, chirping all around.

One does a twirl, another a backflip,
Those aerial dancers, time for a trip!
With noses so big, they make quite a sight,
Belly flops that cause quite a fright.

Kites overhead take lessons in glide,
While speckled rays drift with nothing to hide.
Oh, the comic grace, so silly and bold,
These sea giants surely do as they're told!

Voices of the Mist

Echoes chat in tones so deep,
A surfside convo before they sleep.
Whispers float on twilight's breeze,
As soggy socks tease with little sneezes.

Chirpy calls from under the foam,
Splashing jokes that feel like home.
Mysterious giggles, who could they be?
A shrimp's punchline? Just wait and see!

Seaweed fans twisting with delight,
As barnacle bands play all night.
The symphony carries under the stars,
Making friends with passing cars.

Shadows of Marine Majesty

In the depths, shadows glide with cheer,
Cartwheeling fish, do we dare draw near?
A squid's ink blinks a silly ghost,
While octopuses throw the biggest boast!

With a twist and a flop, the dance does sway,
A luminous light show comes out to play.
All around, the laughter erupts,
As starfish clap their little cups.

The swirl of tail fins paints the dusk,
In bubbles, we trust it's all in good musk.
Those shadows hide chuckles, a merry parade,
In the ocean's embrace, silliness won't fade!

Freedom in the Foam

In the splash and the crash, a silly show,
Fins flap like the hands of a sea-mad pro.
Bubbles dance like they're in a wild race,
While fish all giggle, smiling with grace.

With each twist and turn, the sea critters play,
Rolling and tumbling in a grand ballet.
A dolphin dives deep, then leaps up with flair,
"Catch me if you can!" echoes somewhere in air.

The currents are laughter, the tides pull the fun,
As seaweed wiggles, nudged by the sun.
Whimsical whirlpools swirl round and round,
Where antics of sea life surely abound.

So here's to the frolic and freedom we crave,
In the buoyant blue depths, so hearty and brave.
Let's raise our voices, sing to the tide,
In this swirl of laughter, joy will abide.

Resonance of the Mammoth

Echoes from the past, a rumble so grand,
Like old mammoths swaying in a poppy band.
They trumpet and bumble, they wiggle and sway,
Making up new moves in their own funny way.

A splash and a grunt, a shivering shout,
The frosty sea dancing, there's no doubt.
They glide like fine dancers, in a large parade,
With shiny fish hats, they've got it made!

A walrus with shades lounges by the tide,
While a seal juggles fish with remarkable pride.
Laughter transcends in this watery sphere,
As every great beast has a story to share.

Join in with the madness, float freely and sing,
To the tune of the currents that joyfully ring.
We're the titans of laughter in this oceanic spree,
Where every big wave is a chance to be free.

Guardians of the Deep Blue

Down in the blue, where the otters all glide,
Guardians chuckle with the ocean as their guide.
They wear crowns of coral and laugh at the sun,
Defenders of silliness, they're always on the run.

With cheeks full of krill, they plan a grand feast,
And paint the sea canvas, where joy is released.
A turtle in shades is a wise little chap,
While starfish do yoga, 'Can you do this clap?'

Each creature conspires in this vibrant abyss,
While bubbles are bursting from sheer bliss.
They twirl through the currents, wearing grins so wide,
As laughter bounces off every rolling tide.

So let's join the party, dance under the moon,
Where every fish joins in a jubilant tune.
The guardians gather, with hearts full of light,
In this deep blue kingdom, everything feels right.

Symphony of the Spheres

Under the waves, where music can be found,
Octopuses shuffle to the seabed sound.
With their colorful bodies, a dazzling array,
They lead the parade in a whimsical sway.

The fish form a chorus, with gills all aflame,
Singing the praises of this watery game.
"Let's rock and roll!" echoes through brine,
As crabs do the cha-cha, feeling just fine.

The bubbles keep popping like drums in the air,
While plankton throw parties for the folks unaware.
A show like no other, vibrant and bright,
Where sea creatures rock 'til the fall of the night.

Join in the rhythm, let your laughter flow,
In this symphony vast, with a ceaseless glow.
With every wave crashing, a dance to be shared,
In this chorus of life where all hearts are bared.

Ballet of the Behemoths

In the ocean's grand ballroom, they dance,
Two giants in a waltz, what a chance!
With flippers for arms, they twist and twirl,
Spinning around, giving fish a whirl.

They leap and they splash, oh what a sight,
With each blubbery flip, they bring pure delight.
The seagulls squawk, a raucous cheer,
As these hefty dancers glide without fear.

A pirouette here, a dive and a bob,
Two plump prima donnas, each trying to throb.
They'll take a bow, the audience claps,
While jellyfish giggle in silly mishaps.

And when the curtain falls, they'll take a break,
Sipping on seaweed, for goodness' sake!
The ocean, their stage, for laughter and fun,
With each splash of joy, the show's never done.

Whispering Currents

Bubbles escape with a ticklish sound,
As frolicsome fins spin round and round.
"Hey, did you hear what the kelp just said?"
"Makes me want to swim right into bed!"

The currents chuckle, swaying with glee,
As fish start their gossip like it's a spree.
"Did you see Dave? He tripped on a shell!"
"Oh, not again! That boy can't swim well!"

With tickling waves, they play peekaboo,
Making silly faces, oh can you view?
The laughter erupts, a bubbly delight,
As they sway and sway, in the soft light.

"Let's start a band!" yells a sprightly sprat,
With seaweed tambourines, imagine that!
As bubbles burst forth with each salty song,
The world's underwater giggle, where all belong.

Shadows of the Surface

The shadows drift in, with a playful tease,
Creating wild shapes, like green cheese!
"Is that a whale, or a big swimming chair?"
"Hey look, it's Fred, oh wait, it's a flare!"

The sunlight dips low, like a sleepyhead,
Casting goofiness on the ocean bed.
"Can we catch a shadow? Those silly old things!"
"Only if you have something shiny that sings!"

A game of peek-a-boo with the sunlit blue,
"Hey, watch me vanish, can you see through?"
With giggles and shadows entwined in a twist,
What creatures are hiding? Let's not resist!

"Look out! A buoy, or a floating cat?"
"Nope, just a bubble with a silly hat!"
The ocean's reflections, so wacky and wide,
Swirling in laughter, where dreams collide.

Guardians of the Depths

With flippers akimbo, they patrol the sea,
These hefty protectors, both noble and free.
"Onward, my friends, to the great coral hall!"
"We'll guard this home, no matter how small!"

A mermaid appears with a treasure map,
"Squidward, your jokes, what a lovely chap!"
"Hold tight, swim faster, there's mischief ahead!"
"We'll show those darn sharks, they should be fed!"

"Brush your teeth, brush your fins! What's that smell?"
"It's just your sea sandwich, oh what a swell!"
With giggles and grins, they race through the foam,
Guardians indeed, but at heart, they're home.

In their underwater kingdom, joy is the creed,
Where laughter abounds, and friends take the lead.
So if you should wander down through the waves,
Know the jesters are watching, and oh how they crave!

Ocean's Lullaby

In the deep, a song will play,
Fish and seals dance all day.
Bubbles rise like joyful sounds,
Underneath, the silly clowns.

Splashing water, a comical cheer,
Tails like trumpets, loud and clear.
Whirling 'round in a playful show,
Who knew currents could steal the show?

Stars above twinkle quite bright,
As sea critters act with delight.
A gentle wave dips low to tease,
Swirling laughter rides the breeze.

Gliding with Grace

Floating figures, soft and round,
With a twirl, they hit the ground.
Up in the air, a leap and a dive,
Who knew the sea could come alive?

Belly flops that make a splash,
An acrobat's splashy bash.
Slippery friends with cartwheel flair,
Glide on currents, without a care.

A fin here, a twirl there,
Giggles echo everywhere.
Beneath the sun, under the sky,
Fins and laughter will always fly.

Echoes of the Sea's Heart

Listen close, the ocean giggles,
In secret depths, it shares its wiggles.
A chorus swells, oh what a tune,
While jellyfish waltz with a balloon.

Giant shadows loom and sway,
Making strange shapes in the bay.
They wink and wave with a funny spout,
What are they thinking? Hmm, no doubt!

Bubbles burst like pop balloons,
Currents dance like cartoon raccoons.
With every splash a joyful part,
The sea sings out from its heart.

Legends in the Waves

Once upon a time, they say,
Fins told tales in a silly way.
An octopus wore a dapper hat,
While the crab danced like a tap-tap cat.

Fishermen laughed at tales so sweet,
Of underwater parties – what a feat!
With a wink, they leapt and spun,
Who knew the ocean could be such fun?

Caught in a tide of fishy laughs,
Chasing dreams in playful halves.
As legends bloom from coral beds,
The ocean giggles, and joy spreads.

Gliding Against the Gales

Sailing with a belly full of blubber,
Puffed up with pride, oh what a flubber!
Caught in a gust, oh dear me,
Patting my head, is that even me?

Twisting and turning, a ballet of blips,
Skidding on waves, I'm doing back flips!
Laughter erupts as I dive anew,
Splashing the sailor, oh what a view!

Feeling quite fancy in my salty suit,
Dancing through currents, a big fish hoot!
Nibbling on kelp, a gourmet delight,
With every mouthful, I'm taking flight!

Chasing the tide with a wink and a grin,
Regaling the sea with a joyful din!
Why walk when you can glide, I say,
Let the storm take me, I'll dance all day!

Lullaby of the Leviathans

Deep beneath the shimmering waves,
Snoring like giants, sleeping in caves.
With bubbles and giggles, we slumber deep,
The ocean hums, while we gently creep.

Dreaming of fish who can't swim as fast,
We paddle and play, our shadows cast.
Oh, what a sight, us large and laid back,
Tiptoeing on currents, we'll not fall slack!

Tickling the angelfish, oh how they squirm,
Chasing them round, we waddle and turn.
With a flick of our tails, they scatter and flee,
But our belly laughs flow like a wild spree!

As clouds above puff and churn with delight,
We toss and we tumble like stars in the night.
So here's to the deep where the big ones play,
In a sleepy, silly, aquatic ballet!

Songs of Serene Giants

In the big blue, we croon and we call,
Serenading the sea with a raucous brawl.
Fins flapping wildly, what a sight to see,
Melodies bouncing, oh joy, oh glee!

All the creatures gather for our choir,
Sea turtles tap dance, it never tires.
With bubbles and burbles, we harmonize,
Echoes of laughter under sunlit skies.

Sailors above scratch their heads in dismay,
As we break out into our joyous ballet.
"Are those whales?" they ponder with open jaws,
Not a whale, but a chorus with oceanic paws!

So let's flip and splash in our watery fun,
Singing in unison until the day's done.
For life in the sea is a glorious rhyme,
With song and with laughter, we measure our time!

The Dance of the Depths

Under the waves where the wild things play,
We twirl and we whirl, come dance, they say!
With a jig and a spin, we move to the beat,
A frothy ballet, oh, isn't it neat?

Spinning like tops in a grand ocean show,
Wiggling our tails with a cheeky glow.
Bubbles erupt with a giggling sound,
As we twist and we twine, so joyfully found!

Pirouettes and leaps make the reef burst into cheer,
We're the dancing kings of the oceanic sphere!
With pals 'round our fins, what a splendid sight,
Under twinkling stars, all shimmering bright!

So join in the frolic, don't be shy,
The depths are alive 'neath the boundless sky.
In a flurry of fun, we leap and we glide,
For in the deep blue, we let joy abide!

Flying the Ocean's Embrace

Splash! Flap! A big leap high,
Fish laugh as they swim on by.
Air bubbles tickle, just a tease,
As fins spin like leaves in the breeze.

Wobbling high on the playful tide,
Hiccups of laughter, they can't hide.
Gulls join the dance, with flapping wings,
In this grand show, even a fish sings!

With every flip, a bellyache,
From eating too much seaweed cake.
A porpoise giggles, what a sight,
As ocean's jesters take to flight!

Together they spin, a merry crew,
In this watery realm, joy feels new.
Splashing silly, making waves,
In the ocean's heart, laughter braves!

Beneath the Vastness

Bubbles rise like giggles in air,
A crab cracks jokes, without a care.
Starfish chuckle, flat on their backs,
While octopuses plot hijinks and pranks.

The rumble below is a whale's deep laugh,
Playing hide and seek with the bright sea staff.
A dolphin darts, a trickster divine,
As kelp sways to a rhythm so fine.

With jellyfish floating, glowing like stars,
They dance to the tunes of sea guitars.
Anemones sway with a gentle grace,
While fish form a conga, quick in their race.

Oh, the ocean hums with a comedy show,
The vastness is filled with chuckles and glow.
In every corner, bright laughter rings,
Beneath the waves, joy's what it brings!

Diving into the Whisper

Whispers of currents call out with glee,
As fishy comedians swim wild and free.
Flipping and flopping, a splashy parade,
With barnacles joining, they're unafraid.

A flounder debates, "Who's the funniest here?"
The swordfish insists, "It's me, I'm sincere!"
Turtles roll 'round, with shells full of jokes,
While squid ink sketches of silly folks.

Crabs tap dance on the sandy floor,
With claps of their claws, they're begging for more.
Seahorses giggle, riding the tide,
In this ocean gig fest, let joy be our guide!

So dive with a splash, join the eclectic stew,
In whispers of laughter, here's fun for you.
Embrace the odd, let your worries fly,
In the depths of the sea, the best chuckles lie!

Reverent Roars of the Deep

In shadows and whispers, the deep calls aloud,
A symphony swells, nature's vibrant crowd.
Echoes of giggles, a roguish retreat,
The bass of the waves, a rhythmic heartbeat.

Blubbers and honks from the grand, wise crew,
Each roar is a riddle, intriguing and new.
Seals in the back are throwing their song,
While starfish giggle—'This won't take long!'

Bubbles burst like laughter, bright and eruptive,
As creatures unite in a dance that's productive.
The deep sea feels like a well-stocked joke box,
Swirling and twirling in quirky paradox.

So dive down, dear friend, to where laughter abounds,
Amongst the deep callers, joy spins and sounds.
With reverent roars, let your spirit break free,
In the heart of the ocean, pure glee's the decree!

Ever Present, Ever Free

Flippers flapping in the breeze,
They dance like fish among the trees.
A splash of joy, a giddy show,
With giggles echoing far below.

They hold a party in the sea,
With bubbles forming quite a spree.
Their laughter bubbles up so loud,
While seagulls join, a big, bold crowd.

Whiskers tickle every wave,
Silly antics, oh so brave!
They prance and spin, what a delight,
Making waves in day and night.

In the currents, jesters play,
They twist and twirl in grand ballet.
Forever frolicking with glee,
The ocean's laughter, wild and free.

Wings of the Abyss

With mighty tails, they leap and dive,
Making fish laugh, oh, what a jive!
They wear the sea like a swanky coat,
While jellyfish giggle and float.

They ride the swells, what a sight,
Glide through waters, pure delight.
Sea turtles chuckle at their stunts,
As dolphins join in funny hunts.

Bubbles burst from playful grins,
Silly games for aquatic kin.
The ocean echoes with their cheer,
Join the game, let's all appear!

With every flip, a splashy twist,
They leave a trail of water mist.
A carnival beneath the blue,
Where laughter reigns, and worries few.

Travelers of the Tides

They sail the waves on frothy tops,
With silly hats and little flops.
Packing snacks of seaweed treats,
They journey far with happy fleets.

Their maps are made of colorful coral,
Adventure calls, a joyful brawl.
As currents guide their giddy roam,
Each splash a tale, each tide a home.

From kelp forests to sandy bays,
They share their stories in funny ways.
Their gurgles sound like little chimes,
Rhythmic laughter stealing times.

Around the world, they waddle wide,
Riding waves like a merry slide.
In the ocean's arms, they smile so bright,
The world's a stage in the sun's soft light.

Dawn of the Deep

When the sun peeks, oh what a sight,
Fish wear pajamas, dark and tight.
The ocean yawns, with a misty grin,
As sleepy bubbles rise and spin.

A morning concert, oh, what a treat!
With krill on stage, tapping their feet.
Seals in tuxedos, whales with flair,
A crazy dance in the salty air.

Clownfish giggle, puffers puff,
The depth is bright, where it's never rough.
The dawn brings glee, a vibrant hue,
As sea critters start their debut.

With a flip and a splash, they break the dawn,
Every corner of the sea, they fawn.
The deep is alive, a swirling delight,
A funny show, from day till night.

Nature's Marvels Above the Depths

In the heights where the breezes play,
Giant dancers twirl and sway.
With a splash and a flip, they tease,
Laughter flows like the bright sea breeze.

With blubbery chins, they puff and blow,
Wobbling along in a silly show.
They sing notes that are quite absurd,
Even the seagulls are disturbed!

Bubbles rise like laughter's cheer,
Matching the joy that's felt right here.
While they bask under sunshine's beams,
A circus act born from ocean dreams.

So raise a glass to those seafaring fools,
Mastering the art of aquatic schools.
Nature's wonders, with giggles abound,
In the splashing stages, they're ocean-bound.

Spirit of the Tides

Weaving through salty foam and spray,
With big toothy grins, they play.
Their flippers flail in a wacky way,
Making dolphins shout, 'Hey, let's stay!'

Sailing high on water's crest,
Gurgling giggles, they never rest.
One leaps up and gives a cheer,
A belly flop that draws us near.

With a belly of blubber and a heart of gold,
They cavort and frolic, bold and sold.
In the tide's embrace they find their groove,
Making blubbery dances that always prove.

So let the tides bring their joyous laugh,
As they whirl and twirl on a snappy half.
Nature's jesters beneath the sky,
With each grand leap, they wave goodbye!

Celestial Melodies

Look up high, what do we see?
A band of singers in glee!
With every breach, a chorus loud,
Tickling the ocean, making us proud.

They sing of fish and reefs galore,
Dancing rhythms we can't ignore.
With a splash, they hit a note,
That even the crabs cannot gloat.

Their laughter echoes through the waves,
Bestowing joy that always saves.
As they serenade their ocean kin,
We can't help but join in the din!

In harmony with the sea and skies,
These merry troubadours surely rise.
Bringing whimsy to all who listen,
With sparkling notes that glisten and glisten.

Emissaries of the Abyss

From darkened depths to sunny skies,
These playful giants forever surprise.
With goofy grins and cartwheel feats,
They make currents dance, such silly treats!

Shimmering fins in a whirlpool spin,
Cackling as they dive back in.
They wave at boats, with a cheeky brace,
And make each sailor crack a face.

With every flip, they tickle the tide,
A splashy splash, there's nowhere to hide.
They orchestrate chaos, oh what a sight,
Mischief afloat, by day and by night.

So cheer for the jesters of ocean blue,
They invite us all to join in too.
In their watery world of laughter and cheer,
These roguish ambassadors we hold dear!

Serenades from the Sea

In the belly of a big blue beast,
A fishy choir rehearses for a feast.
With bubbles and tunes, they swim around,
Laughing loud, what a joyful sound!

Jellyfish dance in a sticky parade,
While sea turtles join, all unafraid.
The octopus plays on a saxophone,
Bubbles pop, and we laugh, not alone!

A crab in a hat leads the whole show,
"Clap your claws!" he shouts, "Let's go!"
Seahorses twirl in a dizzy ballet,
Every splash is a giggle, hooray!

The sea stars twinkle, they wink and they grin,
With seaweed confetti, let the fun begin!
In this watery rave, the happy fish play,
And sing to the moon at the end of the day!

Ocean's Symphony

In a splashy suit, the mackerel jumps,
While dolphins work on their silly stumps.
A sea lion juggles with clammy clams,
Making us giggle, oh, what fun jams!

The walrus croons in a baritone,
As sea anemones dance, all alone.
A whale with a kazoo joins the affair,
Blowing bubbles and brushing our hair!

A crab comedy show with slapstick flair,
Pincers clapping, flying through the air.
The otters chuckle in their cozy bay,
Rolling and tumbling, all the day!

Echoing laughs through the waves and the foam,
This symphony plays in our ocean home.
Each splash and each giggle, a song we all share,
In this wild underwater fair!

Echoes of the Blue

In the depths of the sea, hear the giggles arise,
As squids in tuxedos wiggle their ties.
Turtles on skates glide with such grace,
Spraying each other, it's a wet race!

The fish form a band with shells as their drums,
While sea cucumbers march, making fun hums.
Octopus winks with a quirky flair,
Juggling bubbles in the cool salty air!

A clam in a bow tie keeps time with a beat,
Hollers, "Who's next for a funky treat?"
Sea monsters join in, all chaos and glee,
Creating a ruckus, oh, what a spree!

The ocean resounds with laughter and cheer,
As crabby comedians take to the pier.
The echoes of fun fill the briny delight,
In this dazzling dance of the deep-sea night!

Serenade of the Sea Giants

Beneath the waves, big giants cavort,
With flippers and fins, they provide the support.
Big Daddy Narwhal writes pop songs so grand,
They giggle as they twirl, a merry band!

The mighty blue whale gives a deep, hearty laugh,
While cracking fish jokes on a water raft.
The sea serpent spins with a wink and a grin,
Riding the currents, let the fun begin!

Giant squids conduct with a flair for the bold,
While orcas splash colors in blue and gold.
"Join us, dear fish!" they all chant with delight,
In this grand sea serenade, what a sight!

With bubbles of laughter and waves of pure fun,
The giants of sea dance 'til the day is done.
In the great ocean depths, their spirit prevails,
In the bubble-filled waters, joy never fails!

www.ingramcontent.com/pod-product-compliance
Lightning Source LLC
Chambersburg PA
CBHW050308120526
44590CB00016B/2533